"Unlike a real scrapbook, preserving the past, Vivian Mary Carroll's *Talking Leaves Scrapbook* reimagines and reinvigorates us into a vibrant present, where the past is still living and the future was already here."

—ED SKOOG, *author of* RUN THE RED LIGHTS

"The poems of *Talking Leaves Scrapbook* live beyond the page, for after reading, as I walk the world, I find corn pollen on my tongue and hear the many-echoed feathered flutes of history on the wind. These poems teach a new yet ancient sort of sensing. Suddenly at my feet I find all of Carroll's sacred highway muses, those of her ancestors, those of brown corollas, those scrambled jackrabbit toes in the red dirt dust, all below the hung-up splendor of the Milky Way's shine. *Talking Leaves* is more than just a book of scraps but a hymnal of the west, in all its soaking blood and high desert crescent moons. *Talking Leaves* is a fractured sundial of yesterday, now and tomorrow, of you and me and us and them and place and displacement, all played to a beat of the thundered hoofs of all that once ran free and in harmony over this land. Follow Carroll's lattice sky on some stretch of rock and roll and bead-edged buckskin, listen to the talking leaves, find yourself here, feel within these poems everything this here holds."

—ALEXANDER SHALOM JOSEPH, *author of* THE LAST OF THE LIGHT

"*Talking Leaves Scrapbook* is a continuous flash of luminous poetry. Vivian Mary Carroll invites us to enter her poetic chamber through innate phrasing and the sweeping choreography of a camera's eye. She is a heartfelt and grand illusionist. She can draw us into the present moment or leave us lurking in the worn, crystalline halls of memory. Elements of American history are allowed to emerge here too, like sun-faded colors we can still trace across peeling storyboards. There is a contagious joy and appreciation present in this book that I find reminiscent of Allen Ginsberg and Sherwin Bitsui. The agency of the poet is rather astounding, 'Fireplace heat snaps with bluest flames, we swallow pearls soaked in vermouth.' Not a single syllable is wasted."

—CEDAR SIGO, *author of* ALL THIS TIME

TALKING LEAVES SCRAPBOOK

TALKING
LEAVES
SCRAPBOOK

VIVIAN
MARY
CARROLL

Casa Urraca Press
ABIQUIÚ

Set in Cormorant Garamond and Palomino Sans One.

Cover photograph by Betty W. Wolfe.
Author photograph by Jason S. Ordaz.

27 26 25 24   1 2 3 4 5 6 7

First edition

ISBN 978-1-956375-16-9

CASA URRACA PRESS

an imprint of Casa Urraca, Ltd.
PO Box 1119
Abiquiú, New Mexico 87510
casaurracapress.com

For Betty and William.

CONTENTS

I
PALE MEMORIES

HAIBUN FOR BUFFALOES BENEATH A CRESCENT MOON

Sailing west, pitch-smeared timbers slice through salt water. Mirrored full moons scatter like spilled silver coins. Immigrants set foot far from Hudson's River. Dark leaves tremble as winter snows unfurl. The English hunker down, declare Wampanoag land their own. Soon, wagon wheels gouge dry prairie grass. Howls scrape hot across bared teeth. Locusts cloud a blood moon. Firebrands go black. Then, buckskin trophies, feathered and beaded, wither behind museum glass. Drums echo pale memories of first contact's arrogant sin.

White moon lights our dance
Stars pattern beadwork borders
Gift of water flows.

SLOW FALL FLUTE SONG

I came this way.
Veiled eyes newly open
a sky-babe tucked in
a left hand slipping
through the Milky Way
fresh stars whistling
a feathered flute song.

My first smile.
A soft gasp
spotting raven
thermal gliding
above silver water
glistening with
flying fish.

And thunder.
Corn pollen raining yellow.
Raven's shiny eye.
Black wings
greenhouse rising to greet
a hollow-bone
heaven lullaby.

Delivered.
Beyond
a topaz moat onto
a mound of corn.
I sleep and sprout.
Raven downdraft feathers
confetti fall.

RIDING AFTER HER

In a grainy black-and-white movie
   my mother waves
      from a white horse.
She could be Georgia O'Keeffe
   astride a Harley.
Naming me after a bird & flower,
she sprinkled atlas seeds on my eyes,
left blank pages for me to paint.

A sunset journey pulls her away.
Tracing her roots I drive east.

Roadside
   deer-eye daisies nod.
Thistle spikes
   bloom shadows
      across rusted rails.
A red-wing blackbird's
   three-pitch song trills
   time-to-stop, time-to-stop.

Fireflies garland indigo skies.
   Nautilus curved
      my mother sleeps
      on a birch bark bed.

At dawn
   I throttle through pale pink,
music hubbing around an old 8-track.

Chevelle tires spin, clomp, gallop.
Hooves scoop out dust trails.
Hunched to horsehide
   I ride bareback
wind rippling a white mane.

NIGHT TRIP BLUE

Twenty-six corrugated miles
    to Chaco Canyon's
    dark star party.
My car hums a corduroy tune
    fords a sandy wash
    chases dust plumes west.

Curtains of deep marquisette
    unfold   as sunset
    flashes green.
Gatekeepers   coyote
    jackrabbit   kangaroo rat
    lash down   the night.

Starry Cygnus   glides south
    patrolling
    the Milky Way.
Forever gleaming
    Spacelab imitates a
    shooting star.

High desert's night chill
    trusts me
    to seek heat
inside a car buried 'neath
    a mesa's
    inky shadow.

I limbo between leggy pines'
        entwined arms
        arcing the road.
Behind silhouetted tree trunks
        racing headlights
        stalk my path.

At 550's junction
        gas fields glow pale
        companion lights lost.
Two deer rest in dry grass
        heads tracing my passage—
        their hides are blue.

In daylight I return
        there are no deer
        no forest embraces the road.
Unseen, the Milky Way swirls
        a hand reaches out
        snags the echoes
                of blues flying by.

RIPPING THE VEIL

After bobbing for apples
    drowned eyes blink
as two sun dogs blind
    a white sky.

Sifting pond vines for ripe berries,
    an origami crane bites hard,
sharp bill pins retina shine
    chunks down focus
    spits out blur.

Scripted with a
    crow-quill pen
    lemon juice and
    flame
twenty haiku flourish on
    eight quarto pages.

Through dark glasses
    an autumn poet
    on a cold bench
yawns mist
does not hear
    talking leaves
        swirling in the wind
        tapping her shoes.

CHASED LIGHTNING

Something white
dry snow or tears
    scatters
across dark flatlands.
My brown Corolla wagon
    slow dances
partnering Pacific cliffs.
Thunder swings an axe
    thick cedar ribs
    burst.
A cold hand through
an open window
    snatches
radio words
scorched by lightning.
Beneath reflected eyes
a gold tassel
    shimmies.
I climb into who we were
    mismatched
front porch
grad-night dance.

    My rosette gift
    black beaded turtles
    paddling roundelay
    farewells upon your
    pressed white shirt
    third button down.
    You dissolve at dawn
    into six guitar strings
    ten songs
    tobacco embers.

Beneath shrinking
scrapbook tape
faded dime-store
valentines slide.

Four-cylinders scour
a muted city
    layered with
woolen skies, neon puddles.
From a balcony ceiling-high
I view a shallow stage
    you
clothed in Eric Clapton's body.
A dozen fingers bleed
    chalkboard music
a broken symphony
thirsting for snowmelt.
    Outside
lightning escapes across the bay.
    Cars
spray taillight songs.
I step in sidewalk gum
    walk away
marshmallow contrails
    curling
on my tongue.
    Above
a crowning moon
    blushes
for a dance floor's
last couple.

A ROAD UNWINDS

Without a tethering wreath of
    tobacco smoke
I drift through the ceiling

watch for fifty years as
    clay bricks pressed with
rice and obi buttons bake in sun.

On forest moss a young deer's
    hooves spark songs
of pearls and rubies

while rain on a tin roof splatters
    like hot grease crisping
edges of Spam and duck eggs.

I curl in a red dirt blanket
    to calm
cuts that won't scab.

NEEDLE IN GROOVE

Christmas morning whistles snow greetings,
white-eyed grackles ornamenting dark branches.

Soft powder slips through coyote fences,
tapes shadow kisses to scrapbook pages.

Packed inside his denim jacket,
my virgin ink floats tender.

Call me, he says, Texan's two-steps
polishing scuffed oaken floors.

In texts he laughs spun silk,
healed selfie not spelling his name.

Year-end winds erase clouds from skies,
silver-winged cranes swoon through the sun.

Fireplace heat snaps with bluest flames,
we swallow pearls soaked in vermouth.

ARROYO TABLEAU IN DAMP SAND

Hair pollen-tangled yellow
      I sink hiking boots
            into rain erosion.
Sand   scoured wet by night flood
      clumps onto broken branches
            skiffs toward the Rio Grande.

No contrails lattice the sky.

Reserve land yawns
behind three locked gates
      blinks an eye
            shakes a seed pod
            sheds pine needles.

Coffee aroma wisps from an open thermos.

Wet brushes blur images soft
      mountain piñons
            tinted denim
      oak's craggy trunk
            mushroom brown
      ocotillo cane gripped
            by finch toes gray.

I breathe
      morning light
            mirrored upon damp paper
            color bleeding.

CROUCHING INDIAN

Taos blue sky,
    polish squeezed from tubes
    uncapped in Paris salons.
In black-and-white photos, a city artist
    displays teeth, breathes aspen color,
    paints adobe curves & native
    figures clutching blankets.

Easel at attention, brush & palette full,
    he calls upon a muse to render
    a pleasing balance of art & sales.
For twenty-five cents, an Indian model crouches,
    wearing buckskin leggings,
    sometimes with beige thighs bare.

In full-color railroad posters
enticing travelers to Santa Fe,
    the Indian folds himself,
    thighs touching calf.

Come to the Southwest and see:
    a noble savage sips from a water jug,
    a romantic primitive woos a wooden flute,
    a mystic shaman burns ceremonial sweetgrass.
Come see the Redman strike fire,
    plant corn, coil pottery, cook chili.
Come see, touch, poke. Declare to the non-smiling face:
    My grandmother was an Indian, too.

Buy a small clay pot, a beaded trinket, a multi-colored
    headdress, a rubber hatchet.
Let everyone know   you met a real Indian.
    A body not red, but brown.

FLOWERS, A QUICK HISTORY

Flying home,
I scroll images
of frozen light.

Glass flowers, Chihuly honed,
periscope yellow and orange heads
above privet screens.
Thirsty for daylight's heat
they sparkle a sigh, greeting
morning's first tourist.
I aim camera, nod back.
There's a plane to catch.

Not a good map reader
I slip off course, witness
Cheekwood rope and nails
propping exhibit walls,
spot a broken butterfly wing
glued into morning frost,
spy my first red cardinal.
I focus a zoom lens.
He lifts, blurs his image.
I follow.

Green sign unseen among tangled
brush, I drive past Rachel's Lane
then backtrack. In silence,
I walk the mile-and-a-half dirt path to
Andrew Jackson's Hermitage mansion.
Old trees, tall in their power,
stand haughty, leaves unmoving,
like white-haired generals
commanding attack.

My brown Cherokee self
climbs into Old Hickory's
slave wagon to view
empty cottonfields, stone
foundations of slave quarters,
an old well, the still-standing
cabin of Alfred, a favored slave.
I snap familiar guinea hens,
a garden like mine blooming
red zinnias and crested coxcomb,
painted-lady butterflies
sipping yellow nectar.

Cruising souvenir shelves
I choose a lowkey refrigerator
magnet showing Jackson stone-
still atop a white horse.
I hadn't known him as
Indian Killer or
Sharp Knife,
but as a man tugging
at a bandaged soul,
entombed in his own garden
beneath a patinated dome,
forever beside his wife, Rachel.

He loved the same flowers
my Indian mother planted.
So, I nodded farewell
instead of spit.

II
LEATHER WRAPPINGS

CLUTCHING BLANKETS

nvgi aditla tsunilosvhi

The first time
    we walked
corn and trees bubbled
      beneath waters
slapping at mountains' chests.

We walked again,
    leather wrappings,
        blankets,
    crusted with damp snow.

We walked.
    Ice chunks choked rivers.
We walked.
    Wet juniper not holding fire.
We walked,
    until soil beneath sun
      sprouted green.

Roots burrow as deep
    as plants grow tall.

We sing.
We feast.

nvgi aditla tsunilosvhi - Cherokee: "From four directions
                         they arrived."

JUANITA, I HONOR YOUR CHOICE

After Emil Bisttram's "Pueblo Girl"

Black hair   shorn to chin
    speaks of the road you walk
treading miles
    moccasins white   no stain.

Tender sunlight
    skims   your cheeks
    plain   clothing   color   fades.

A hand-stitched   tear
    'tween collar points
a throat-notch   thumbprint
    to cradle
        a golden cross.

Your soft glance
    affirms dancing motes
murmurs   of distant songs
    in   a forgotten tongue.

Juanita
    leaving your pueblo home
        mourn only a little.
Old-world   bells   toll
    supping on your spirit's call.

Left ring-finger   pressed
    you become the squeeze
        and release
the heart-blood   pulse
    of flesh   soul
        faith.

PROVENANCE

A ragged odor
of baked dust & sun
    rises   stale
when I crawl across
the bench seat of
a broken-down
1943 Plymouth coupe.

Centered behind
steering wheel glass
a golden ship
buoyed on etched waves
winks a sail at my toddler eyes.

I flail at foamy water
my breath bubbling.
Ophelia, no.

Silhouette painted green
another ship motors west
crests highways
hauls cargo to seed
the land.

Their offspring sing
    April's tame showers
    grow May's bestest flowers.
I look out a class window
weighing untaught truths about
    broken treaties.
Did not living on a rez
    pale my blood?

After a stray
        enters our yard
and mangles
        a chicken
my mother teaches me
        about anger.
It's not the dog's fault,
she says,
somebody
didn't feed it right.

PONY RIDES

Is it chance or god hand
that strings
    genetic beads
spins
    coded coils
into a spirited
    brown-and-white
Indian pony?

In a found photo
a glum child
    buckled in
rides a painted pony
    plodding a circular rut.
She blinks at
rhinestones flashing on
    a cowgirl shirt
lay-a-way forgotten.

On a northern drive
two pastured horses
    one white
    one brown
steal her eyes.
She sketches them
nostrils sunk into
    juniper mash
    cholla bud wine.
Rearing
    hooves crush
    a citrus sun.

At trail's edge
his mane
    blazed with sky
a pinto strikes at
    dust devils
ghosting up from
    San Lorenzo Canyon.
A woman shifts in
    the saddle.

PECOS WIND DREAM

Snowmelt sparkles Pecos River cold.
Evergreen's sentry raven barks an alarm.
My raised hand grazes heaven's crust.

Parched mud walls
five ceilings high glitter under
cauldron sun's ladled gold.

Dust-swirls scale kiva ladders.

Beside me
bronze messengers
grip knotted cords.

Silent chollas drop yellow fruit.

Glistening shadows swoop like
red macaws, waking revolt
village to village.

I cannot follow.

Grasses dance bloodless in wind
bearing seeds to barren ground.

MILLENNIUM FULL MOON

Tracking clues on
your posted photos
I find where you live.
You are so bad, you say,
a coyote fence between us.
You open the gate anyway.
I learn to pour bourbon,
pale ale chasers.

High-desert moon
spies white above us.
I sink deep into your bicep,
inhale burnt chollas,
scarred husks of
five grand pianos set ablaze.
A musician's creative madness
cooled by a single red
extinguisher.

We were almost the same.
Big-band rhythms swung
my grandparents around
a USO sprung floor.
I discoed in amniotic glitter.
Playing a cardboard guitar
strung with butcher's twine
scratched my musical rash.
What was the real thing like?
A transmitted kiss to the temple
from your radio songs told me.
Every dial swirled to magnetic
north and I followed.

Nine concerts. Sixteen. Twenty-three.
The glory of counting coup fades.
Music is your woman.
A New Year millennium show
borders my home state.
Snow dusts leather jackets.
White muffles a torn bus ticket.
Broken pieces inside a Mason jar
slow a beating pulse.
I archive your emails.

EMPTY LONELY

Crossroads point south
at Galisteo's steeple
fingertips derail
    cd music
flat tire collapses
    slaps.

Raven wings
    flap black
eclipse evening
    tree colors.

Darkness
    casts all
    empty
    blind
like a hip bone's
    gaping eye,
the dry maw cry
of a missing cat,
    mummified shadow
    uncovered
        in wild grasses
        sprouting seed.

Mile marker 53
    basin between hills
flip phone dead.
Yellow hazard flash
    flagging
    rescue.
Lonesome flies on bat wings
    into indigo
    skies.

ON A SPACESHIP SOMEWHERE

Behind my forehead a movie flickers.
I'm Barbie-tiny in flowered flares.

Stratosphere-high my airship hovers
plotting movement of wandering stars.

Touching down on Taos mountain
I spy your offering in Mabel's labyrinth.

After inventing mango sorbet
I lasso you from a tar paper roof.

Exchanging horsehead nebula theory,
you ask if extraterrestrials really exist.

My projector jumps, film sprockets tear.
Your bow-tie smile spools to the floor.

IN YOUR DREAMS DO I SMILE?

On your first tour
    I sped through five counties
        to see you.
Standing next to the stage
    I worried
        you wouldn't find me.
Daring to fix your old hurts
    I booked tickets for bus, plane and train,
    traveled five states in fourteen days
        to hear you sing my name.

Do I ever cross your mind?

Getting lost on tiny roads
    not stopping at faded villages
        weighing directions at railroad junctions.
I don't even remember the name
    of that Indian casino up north—
        a meet-and-greet view
        with stars poking pure
            in the blackness of nowhere.

All you did was hold my hand.

No longer seventeen
I should be over you now,
    past being swept off my feet.
I never look the way I feel
    in photographs of us.
Am I peering through eye holes of a mask?

Who do you see when you look at me?

Cigarettes and cheap snacks.
Night wind perfuming river gorge.
Parking lot littered with aluminum leaves.
Snow drift to mid-thigh.

You say you've seen me
        in cities I've never been.
Is this your dream or mine?
Stage lights dim.   Curtains part.

I refold my memory map,
        jockey it back
                into the glove box.

SAINT IN POCKET

Kateri Tekakwitha
with each squeak of a mission's
prayer-card rack your Haudenosaunee
name sings white lilies. I pay pennies
to pocket your unscarred likeness,
calm in buckskin and beads,
braided hair backlit halo gold.
I am random and reckless.

Gah-deh-lee Deh-gah-gwee-tah.
Sleeping on thorns led to your path.
Even with bad eyesight you leaned
into wind and snow for two months,
treading two hundred miles through shadowed
woods, across icy rivers, to receive
First Holy Communion
on Christmas Day.

A Christmas Eve babe
brown skin bearing three pock
marks, I, too, travel solo.
I sit apart eating airport fig bars,
listening not to music I follow
but to baggage wheels wobbling
over tile grout.

Without direction I've lost my way
in wheat fields picking wild bluebells.
I've exited unmarked transit doors
at night, rushing down wrong streets in
rainy San Francisco dark.

From a window, a blue-black ocean
tickling the toes of a fading sun
stirs a lonesome burn inside me.
I cling to Mona Lisa's smile.
Am I on the right subway platform?
Will the muse bless me this time
with a healing bandage?

A gift of bubblegum slides into
my levi pocket. I touch your portrait.
I grow weary, *Gah-deh-lee.* Sing me home.

III
DIRT SHORTCUT

STRAW BOYS

I pedal a green two-wheeler,
fat 24-inch tires squishing into
July's hot tar-and-gravel road.
Ahead, my sister's slender capri legs
pump her narrow tires fast, faster,
sprocket teeth eating through chain.
Speed snaps and jerks
the beaded coin purse
dangling from a leather strap
around her wrist.
She knows I can't catch up.

My handlebars edge
a field of blazing wheat
buckling in summer's breeze.
Inside swaying heads, ripe
kernels chatter like
red-eye cicadas.
Sister's bike shudders past
bare-limbed peach trees,
jets down a dirt shortcut
toward Palmateer's market.

I shove my rear pedal down,
braking, front tire kissing
black-and-white high-tops
stretched across a dry ditch.
Elmer squints pale eyes
behind wire-frame lenses.
Six years earlier we rode
the same squat yellow bus
to kindergarten.
How ya been? I ask.

Inside a "Gimme Shelter" t-shirt
one knobby shoulder bobs
like a red apple in water.
He lifts a dented beer can,
litter from a passing car.
Wheat straw pokes out
a church key bite.
The taste is warm, amber.

At the kitchen table I clip an obit
from the *Daily Journal*
detailing the death of
Elmer's Marine brother
in a far away place called
Khe Sanh. I show it to
my mother. She nods,
says nothing about the
sourdough scent of beer wafting
like flies around my hair.

One knee bloody, Sister
slams the screen door,
hollers how I left her
waiting at the market.
On her way home,
a dusty pickup truck
had crept up behind her
blaring its horn inches away
from her red reflector.
Sister tumbled to the blacktop,
bike basket mangled,
bread flattened, milk carton
contents spreading white.

Hay and straw sifted
from the passing truck bed,
the driver's laughter also
scattering down the road.

I stand behind my mother
as she inspects Sister's knee.
No one mentions her teen
crush on the young driver
or shares news of his recent
enlistment. My stomach slips
realizing I prefer Sister's rage now
than her racked tears when
she'll read a future list of war dead.

SNIPER

Bloodless moon
   glowing full
betray not my nesting site
     hangs
   above leaves.

Black pajama
   river flotsam
wet weapon strapped close
     glides through
   dank water
     below.

Jungle sweat scalds
   dry eyes
don't blink.

Feel winter's sting on skin
  a snowball breaching
  your childhood ice fort.

Stagnant ripples
        sink to silence
don't   *breathe.*

Faces   webbed
        in crosshairs.

Index triggers   squeeze.

Red lava
        cracks
                black water.

Bobbing up
        I float.
                Jetsam.

COASTLINE DANCING

Being neither draftee
    nor eager volunteer
I have no hash marks to sew
    from the sixties'
    swinging love army.

A flushed-cheek schoolgirl tale
smells of pink bubblegum,
deep-red, Vienna, velvet clouded in
    his cigarillo smoke
    a chaste balcony peck
    a crooked smile.

A foggy autumn tango
in a Berkeley eucalyptus grove
sings with dried leaves
crumbling beneath our
    gliding feet.

From a Pacific amphitheater
    parking lot
we dodge lightning hooves of
    magenta stallions
piercing twilight clouds.
Neon canyon nights taste of
    dissolved pearls
hissing with
    whiskey's burn.

A lamppost on guard duty
my gaslight eyes
    cast off sleep.

Pale dawn
    sulks.
Empty hunger nibbles
    cold toast
spread with
    a hardened heart.

TINY NAIL

Beneath a white moon
    powder soft snow
        glows on a shed roof.

Morning sun's crucible
    slides icicles over eaves
        crunches tender beads underfoot.

Cat kibble raining into a pie tin
    calls four ferals to the shed door.
        A sparkling shape glints for my eyes.

I lean close. A fresh spray of
    yellow elm leaves cradles
        a crystalline horseshoe nail.

Should I or should I not
    pick up the miniature find?
        A cat head-bumps my glove.

In my hand the tiny nail
    would breathe body heat
        bleed liquid into leather.

I stand minus treasure,
    cats silent, warming my boots.
        An icicle tip breaks loose.

Without looking I see
    a matching moonstone hammer
        lying on a brown leaf.

COME SEE THE ELEPHANT

Little solo girl-girl
    cut Vegas loose
short-skirt hem shimmy
    shiny kid-shoes
nickel-bucket payout
    lucky slot win
after-concert dinner
    loose change for tip.

Post concert, one a.m.
cigar smoke and cowboy hats
    girl scorches beside
        a Texas gambling man.

He tips his fist
she breathes in luck.

she don't know the rules
of this dicey game.

girl can't run
    glaciers calve into purest blue
girl can't run
    brain honey leaks whitest diamonds
girl can't run
    hummingbird throat pulses ruby
    needle beak weaves an emerald gown
    feather cape sweeps run-away stones.

Go, girl, go, go.
    Run.

RIBBON DOG SUMMER

An oak canopy shades a child
hugging a thorny hedge.
Her face
    her yellow party dress
pearl with honeysuckle dew.

Four tea-kettle guinea hens
scrabble across a soft tar road.
Through dark greenery
she watches them hone on a yellow house
    coated with climbing vines.
This isn't where I live.

Momma's dream dogs, pretty in ribbon bows,
are not wagging behind a weather-gray gate.
I think I'm lost again.

A finger jabbing thorn
    primes her legs for flight.
She darts from sable shadows
    into kaleidoscope heat.
Her ears pool hot blood
    hearing again
    a lazy summer story
Momma tells of
    chattering dogs in ribbons
walking beside her on
    a birthday party path.
I've got to find that party.
I'll be late again.

HARVEST FAIR

Narrow blacktop slices through prairie grass.
Fender jetstream rattles dry seed pods.
Wild harebell songs ripple uphill.

Red-speckled cattle graze beside creek beds.
From ridgeside, velvet pronghorn rumps
look like large creamy flowers.

A tank full of blue sky
flows down to valley orchards
source of prize plum preserves.

Petting zoo animals nibble toddler toes.
Dizzy rides grind gears, cry calliope tears.
Perfuming the night, hotdogs and cinnamon rolls.

Topple tin ducks, cuddle home a teddy bear.
Across dark skies, chrysanthemums explode pink and gold.
Lazy cars roll home, headlights nudging at sleepy night.

SEVENTH DAY OF CHRISTMAS

Dry pine needles
      escape to
      an Anchorage floor.

Eastern roof icicles
      hold tight with
      crystal smiles.

New Year's Eve fireworks
fog blotted   pop
      whistle   sight unseen.

January mid-morning horizon
      fills Horus' right eye.
A snapped hockey stick
      bleeds frost
nods its headache amongst
      empty energy cans.

Snow crystals whorl against glass
      like tiny swans sailing.

CHAMISA IN SOFT RAIN

I watch gray rain flush arroyo sand
    around piñon roots
        sink into ruts
            vanish.
Yellow chamisa clings to steep banks.

Crowned with cotton
    low nimbus clouds
    thunder with black-and-white horses.
I see myself hemming a dress
    found in my mother's closet
    as fish-eye pearls
        wash down a drain.

I packed the oatmeal cookies
    we baked
    sprinkled   with honey pollen
        instead of secrets.

After one slow dance you turned,
    exiting beneath a blinking red sign.

CHEROKEE SEVENS

1) Star
light
  mu-
  sic
    cra-
    dle
      song.

2) An-
i-
mals
  once
    spoke
    to
    us.

3) Their
gift:
  se-
  ven
    logs
    for
    fire.

4) Sil-
ver
  winds
    car-
    ry
      me
      high.

5)   I
swim

        be-
        yond

                sun's
                e-
                cho.

6)   Dive
deep

        in-
        to

                dark

                        wa-
                        ter.

7)   On

        tur-
        tle's

                back

                        I
                        ride
                        home.

IV
EYES FORWARD

QUERCUS

A long American car brakes
near the shade of a dark oak
where we wait.

I pull straight like my mother,
shoulders back, eyes forward.
Lowering my lashes

I make the little market
across the two-lane road
shiver like mirage heat.

From a rolled-down window,
a blurry man in a damp shirt
tells us the bus to town
won't come for a long while.

My mother doesn't answer.
She read the bus schedule.
The man drives away.

I am six.
I've experienced kindergarten.
I pretend we weren't sprayed

with words about savages
standing too long in the sun
to know what's good for them.

My mother stands strong.
I raise myself higher
in proud nickel likeness.

quercus - Latin: oak.

FALLING FROM A SEA OF STARS

Six feet from the ground,
in light blue leotard and white tights,
I glide along a tightrope.

Focus not where you're standing but on the point you're walking toward.

Without fear, I skim air, grasp thin memories of childhood—
living outside my body, head buoyant on calm seas.
I see her, peripherally, nine years old, colt legs, plaid dress from Sears,
black-and-white saddle oxfords, white socks.
I search for a key to unlock our separation,
hear an answer in Debussy's "Arabesque #1."
Tomita's synthesizer whistles.
Violins sweep backwards, fanning out like broken-in playing cards.

Sucked through a vacuum I gain warp five
weightless.
Marrow dissolves into glitter.
Chocolate sauce dribbles over French custard ice cream.
Third eyelid filters iridescent forests of frozen stars.

I see her swimming, down, through a lake of funhouse mirrors.
Take my hand, she calls, palms reaching across mist.
A loose grosgrain ribbon unleashes wavy hair.

My nebulous eidolon, sprite, missing left-handed self—
A ride, please, around-and-around Milky Way's carousel.

Her laughter sparkles like mountain snow melt
    rippling over a granite streambed,
    tickling spears of willow branches.

Two steps away, the dismount platform waits.
Shall we? she asks. *Oh, yes,* I answer.
    Arms upraised, we style and bow,
        then tumble head-first.
Waters splash blue without bubbles.

DOUBLE CROCHET RHYTHMS

the south-bound San Joaquin
    shoulders
    a valley wind
steel wheels
    slice iron rails
    cross creosote ties
train windows judder
    over rusty bolts.

my crochet hook
    flashes
silver rhythm
    yarn over
        pull through.
pink loops
        pull through.
breathe in
    breathe out.

vineyards
    clack by
horses graze
    skein   scrolls.
yarn over
    loop
    pull through
again
    repeat
        repeat.

one baby bootie
    breathe in.
repeat
    breathe out.

EYES OF A DESIGNATED ROLLER

Celebrating Independence Day
    summer theater's tech crew
spits watermelon seeds into Pacific mist.
From scrap-lumber frames
Catherine Wheels
    whirl yellow sparks
    into the night's chill.
Trundled onto a fog-dampened lawn
Lady Liberty and an upright piano
    warm the night
    blessing America.

Running late the morning after,
I score two dozen of Peg's
    fresh French crullers
an offering to cut short
the costume shop manager's
    tongue clicking.
Above the cork board,
the Conservatory clock's
hour hand flings itself
    toward nine a.m.
I scribble my initials onto
    the day's sign-in sheet
as an office runner's hand
    yanks away the list.
Snatching a black-edged invitation
    off the board
I hustle from building to building
    pink pastry box
    wafting sugar aroma.

Invitation:
Another opening-night cast party
    begging a hotbox girl's
    special service.

Party:
leading lady picks her molar,
    sucks a second knuckle
    into red-gloss mouth
pout smeared with
    ranch dressing.
Bare-chested bouncer
head topped by a
    bellhop's monkey hat
ejects non-theatrical
    gate crasher.
Two male dancers fold themselves
    into a busy coat closet,
closing an unlatching door
    behind them.

From a sequined bib pocket
    I extract Zig-Zag papers
display my praise-sung rolling talent—
    tight sticks of
        Acapulco Gold
    mixed with heady
        oregano
        and catnip.

BUTTERFLY CROSSING

Hurricane buffeted
    three thousand miles off-course
a figure-eight flutterer
    topples
    on Dorset sand
orange scales
    pale
    still wings
      brittle.

I fly transatlantic
    board two red buses
spy a brick house with
    iron fence
    open bay windows
    perfumed blossoms—
I don't stop.
You might not be home.
It might not be your house.

In a rented Mews flat
    I sip honey tea   slip
into cosmic dancer's skin,
    pose
      back arched
      foot in hand,
balancing a
    butterfly's heart
      floating
    the length
    of me.

Red petals part
    tongue tastes
    amber beads.

STILLNESS OF REMEMBERING

Gold braid unwinds
     from a toreador's cape.
Threads drift soft from
     a sixth-floor
     balcony
dissolve in headlights blaring
     sequins and lamé.

At midnight
     cardboard models,
draped in wine-stained
     silk blouses,
step from toe-pinching
     glass slippers,
slide earnings
     into curbside meters.

Cruising Sunset
     we see our clavicles
     shining white
in neon window reflections.
We ache to match
     Grauman's cement
     shoe prints.

Dawn's toreador bows
     offers a waltz
a shot of peach schnapps.
We toast to
     strangers who
     exchange letters.

TO CHIPPEWA FALLS FAIR

Echoing cries of a carnival wheel,
lost words and music
     circle a silver moon.

Starlight eyes peer down.
Seven Sisters drip mercury
     onto rooftops
     into a closed pickup cab.

Narrow roads north cut through
     dew-faded towns
     fields of tasseled corn.
Airwaves report top prices
     for feeder hogs.

After a five-dollar sneeze of gas
he unpockets tip-jar coins
     orders truck-stop coffee
     and a jelly doughnut.
For her, he gets
     red-eye gravy
     and a biscuit.

Waiting at a formica table
she fingers chords on an air guitar
     pens lyrics on a rough paper towel:

fifty dancing half-moons
     smeared on window grease
hug me with your eyes, sweetheart
     sunset's flashing green
salty tears don't matter none
     heartbreak's done buried me
paint this on my wooden cross—
     "I used to be somebody."

WINGS

Coveted junior high jewelry
        sister's
                cheap souvenir ring
           given as a gift by a friend.
Tropical orange   tangled
             with blue
        butterfly wings
                cut   to fit
                      under
        a small glass dome.

Broken   pained
        wings cry to fly home.

A northern artist
        offers necklace pendants
online   fashioned
        from real dragonfly wings
                found on her farm
                naturally dead.

Their lifespan is short.

Young women
        in red dresses
        some deep ruby
                like hummingbird gorgets
dart behind fallen trees
        lost.

Tiny birds   hover
          green wings
                    shimmering light
softening the sleep of
          summer-skinned women
silent   tender girls
                    left cold and torn.

Found
          unnaturally dead.

APRIL GATHERING, TAOS

Pigment thick
    with caught breath,
bristles stroke
    gold aspen leaves
boughs bleed off canvas
    before piercing
      blue sky.

Silver shadows
    weave silken tendrils,
painted wind
    whistles down
      distant mountains.

Horse and rider
    anchor
      gesso border,
magpie trio
    scoops puddle mud
      with yellow bills.

Imagery
    metaphor
eye rhythm
    movement
color
    speaks.

GRAVE UNKNOWN

My mother plants her good hard shoes
in the airy lobby of my storefront theater,
watching me match artists' name cards
with the asking prices of surrealist paintings
to be auctioned off opening night.

Your father died, she blurts.
Really? I ask.

Social Security phoned.
His account was now hers.

When did he die?
I laugh at the irony when she says,
Around Columbus Day.

After forty-two years of marriage he'd wanted out.
After decades of sweating in fields
and orchards, he wanted his money—
to spend on drink and gambling.
Women, maybe.
He told me once he went to the Philippines
and married another woman.
I never told.

He wasn't Cherokee like my mother and me.
Otherwise, he wouldn't have
touched me like he did.

I go on matching names to images.

V

CALMING SALVE

A FLOWER IN WATER

For the upset child,
Carl Linnaeus, surname
fashioned after the garden's
giant linden tree,
flowers are his only
calming salve.
As a nobleman,
Carl von Linne selects
Linnaea borealis,
twinflowers blooming
on separate tines
anchored upon one stalk,
as his coat-of-arms.

Young Linnaeus studies
the crosshairs of petals,
stamens and pistils,
divides nature by
similarities   not differences.
A man speaks
        a monkey does   not.
Within two weeks
a doctoral degree is his.

Passion fails to save
a drowning friend.
In night dreams he
plunges into salt water
grasps slick caudal fins.
His canal-soaked manuscript
swirls   swift   elusive.
A gray whisper dives
beside him.

After strokes
harvest his memory
he slips beneath the shadow
treads canal waters—
   splash   ripple
      fin   scale
go deep
    deep
       deeper.

PRESERVING SEASONS

Pocketed for a later
    carousel spin
a brass ring sings
    a verdigris song.

Foiled perfume sample
    dry upon opening—
nothing to daub behind ear lobes
    or kiss a warm wrist pulse
nothing to greet confetti rain
    of New Year chiming in.

Red wrapped chocolate hearts
    saved in a Valentine box
        ripen white
    waiting to grace
        a doilied dish.

Late summer—
    gloved hands
    gather cactus pears.
Scrape garnet fruit
    boil   purée
strain red crystal
    into jelly jars.
Keeps for one year
    on a dusty shelf.

DEER AND DRAGONFLY

Hilltop green al fresco dinner done
I escape chatter of mingling souls
        sit beneath umbrellaed leaves
coax my black cat
                by answer machine
to end his under-bed sulking.
His head gash did not
        stitch in perfect line.
It itches, he mews.

A dragonfly just landed on you,
        a fellow student calls.
I think it means good luck.

I might fly home early,
        I tell my cat.

Hillside grasses whisper
tall blades kiss
        a silent deer's
                shoulder.
Cinder-block gray like the low fence
        guarding her trail
the doe sinks
        each hoof
                into uphill tracks
gains high twilight
                where a yellow sun
                        still shines.

A good omen,
        a poet's red lips
                pronounce.
Dark eyes soak into me
        probe palm lines
        decipher skull bumps.
Send me your poems, she says.

I call the answer machine again,
watch   as two dragonflies
        carry the fringe
        of the poet's trailing scarf.

NOWHERE ELSE

Late Autumn's stars, Libra,
dance a song of balance
    above dry corn stalks.
Inside, vinyl ballads
    scale silver notes
    through frosty skies
        past the Pleiades.
    Lullaby
for another groove in time.

    At five p.m., the county fair's
    afternoon country music concert
    over, I asked for an autograph,
    and wouldn't he care to escape
    the sun-baked valley, laying low
    on ten delta acres cooled by evening
    breezes and irrigation mist?
    A carousel's tinny organ
    rippled with the heat.

On back porch steps again,
    a closeness skin
    remembers,
we listen as walnut leaves scud
    down a gray roof
    scatter onto a patchy lawn.
He'd found my delta town by
tracing rural California
    spread across two folds
        of a splitting roadmap.

His truck had turned off
    the levee road
    onto my gravel drive.
I'd tripped at the sound
    ripping fringe off
    my Stevie Nicks shawl.
Backlit in high beams,
    toddler in arms,
he handed me
    all the years that passed.
I had nowhere else to go.

His watch beeps.
Inside, my mantel clock echoes
    a muted warmth
a granny-squares crocheted blanket
    hugging his sleeping child.
A lost shadow rides across his face.
He has the same clock back home.
Libra dips behind papery corn leaves.

I yawn. *Coffee?*
He catches the screen door.
Got anything stronger?

SOMETIMES WORDS WON'T DO

Peach roses show deep appreciation.
Eleven roses announce:
    I'm truly, deeply loved.
Imagine
if I returned your sweet bouquet
    affection's proof not needed.
Suppose I pried from shed walls
rusty horseshoes you'd nailed in
crescent formation
    keeping luck from flowing out—
pitched them in senior games instead.

What if I no longer paused to bathe
    brave and cold
'neath starry Milky Way skies
nor listened to dawn's bird-song
forecasting days clear of gloom?
If I said pink tulips tasted like cotton candy
    would you promise to agree?
I may adore tribal cloaks hand-tied with
    feathers waxen and rare,
but for you
I'll cancel Icarus' flight lessons citing
    an inability to swim.

Imagine I grasped carousel's ring,
	crunched stir-fried bodies of gods,
invited the Gorgon mother for dinner,
	cooed at an unwrapped gift blender,
insisted she eat first
using our one faux silver fork.
We've battled broken windmills
channeled
	a rich life
beyond gifts of garnets,
	jade, lapis lazuli.
Would we be so blessed if
we hadn't
	laughed in spring rain or
	waltzed in fresh snow or
smiled as we embroidered
	the moon?

SPACIOUS SKIES

Trailing Willie Nelson
courthouse workmates
map north to rainy Puyallup.
Lime-green VW bug
skates highways
to fairgrounds where
outlaw country gals
hunker on wet concert chairs
draped garbage-bag black.

Pacific beach morning
patterned by ebbing waves
two gals search
for sand dollars.
No white doves soar from
empty skeletal pates.

Bumping air
pelicans scoop frayed mist.
Kelp strands die entangled.
Upriver, paper-mill fumes
blot feathery ghosts
winging a flyway home.

Waves peak, sink,
bend earth's horizon,
jockey garbage to shores.

Buckled in flight,
one gal cushions six sand dollars
screwed in a green Mason jar.
The other tracks Willie's tour bus
hungry for more french-fried exhaust.

BUCKLE BUNNY BLUES

Inside his ribcage a compass spins,
    turning the wheels of his faded truck.
No money, no buckles, not even loser's luck—
    rodeo back-number his only souvenir.

    At home his Lady scrubs linoleum scars,
        stages a welcome home surprise:
    chickens fed, cows milked, house cleaned,
        cheap wedding band cradled in a shiny sink.

Mile markers blur on white desert highways,
    a magnetic arrow stuck on a setting sun.
Evangelical static folds into border palabra,
    no radio anthems of cowboys bred for pain.

    Lady's boots kick up dust blossoms
        as she scuffs an old levee road.
    Valise at her side, thumb out for a ride,
        she's packed his gold buckles to pawn.

Two-lane hiking since the truck broke dry,
    his tongue licks salt, sweat and brew.
A few fields home, pheasants clatter corn;
    sunblind, he sees Lady running with open arms.

MORNING AT MABEL DODGE LUHAN'S

Last leaf's winter shadow—
 a dark bird glides down,
sorts CrackerJack toys, old flowers, coins,
 offered in silence.

Parapet perched, ceramic roosters eye
 empty pigeon houses,
stare at faded prayer flags hanging slack
 with bearded dew.

Early-riser walks labyrinth's
 spiral rhythm.
Behind him, Taos Mountain
 swallows morning's white moon.

LEAVE THE SUN BEHIND ME

Scrapbook pages rarely turned
newsprint dots photo-dated
    some bright fireflies
    some tarnished stars.
Concert reviews
    taped from behind
headlines fresh not yellow.
Celeb face collages,
fashion trends
    never sewn
    never worn
person I never was.

Who I was
sister's cool shoes slipped on
thirty-five-cent bus fare to town.
Mercury falling.
Memories
    Instamatic squares,
brick auditorium background,
Brit band images with
bubblegum card
    trading value.
Tugged by a jingle-jangle
    guitar song
I'm sucked through
    a galaxy
    as black as
empty scrapbook pages.

        I watch
a setting sun brush gold on
        tree leaves,
burnish red
        the breasts of cranes
flying beneath
        a crescent moon.
I wave
as one crane peels from
        chevron lines
turns north
        to find the heart-mate
not gliding beside him.

LAYING A BREATHLESS BODY TO REST

Turtle shells pray
     shhush-shhush-shhush-shhusha
pebbles in their bellies sing
     shhush-shhush-shhush-shhusha.

When last breath-*sshush-shhush-*
     escapes in sleep-*shhush-shhushaaa-*
          does it dive deep,
               slide down stalactites,
                    seek cellophane fire
                         that crackles and melts?

Does last breath-*shhush-shhush-*
     burst high-*shhush-shhushaaa-*
          a fireworks tail,
               an asterisk winking,
                    pinwheel light sparkling,
                         raining soft gold?

After last breath-*shhusha-*
     we bury body's husk-*shhush-shhusha-*
          hair washed in sun's light,
               to sleep without weeping,
                    to breathe like the wind blows—
                         shhush
                         shhush
                         shhush
                         shhusha.

ACKNOWLEDGMENTS

To these gracious publications I offer heartfelt thanks for introducing the following poems to the planet:

Institute of American Indian Arts Student Anthology: "Cherokee Sevens," "Falling from a Sea of Stars," "Riding After Her," "In Your Dreams Do I Smile?"

New Limestone Review: "Pony Rides," "Arroyo Tableau in Damp Sand," "Butterfly Crossing."

New Mexico Poetry Anthology 2023: "Night Trip Blue."

Tribal College Journal: "Laying a Breathless Body to Rest," "Quercus."

Yellow Medicine Review: "Clutching Blankets," "Crouching Indian," "Flowers, a Quick History," "Haibun for Buffaloes Beneath a Crescent Moon," "Morning at Mabel Dodge Luhan's," "Wings."

To infinite Time, I return many thanks for the manner in which experience is enfolded with memory, resulting in colorful words and imagery. These become like sequins and beads, sewn into poetry to provide an inner light.

To family, friends, and mentors, I offer enormous blessings and thank-yous. Without the life-long love and encouragement from my mother, Betty, and my husband, William, I could not have fully realized the magic and beauty of forming language into poetry that I am now able to share with others. I dedicate this book to both of you.

To Suzy Rouiller, Beverly Mobley, Peter Starren, Robbin Ware, Dr. Leona Zastrow—I am grateful for your abundance of kindness and honesty in support of my writing.

To the welcoming bands of friends who warmed various stages of my life and whom I trusted to read my writings, I blush with gratitude for your presence in shaping my work: Leslie Benoy, Teresa Chamberlain, Lilly Kennedy, Victoria Gonzales Clay, Linda Smock, Rachelle Pablo, Chris Owens, Alexander Shalom Joseph, Wayne Yandell, Jennifer O'Neill Pickering, Nancy Schoellkopf.

To the fierce mentors, teachers, and workshop leaders who masterfully extracted tears and putty from a guarded heart without breaking my spirit, I am indebted for your gifts to dig deeper and push further: James Thomas Stevens, Sherwin Bitsui, Joan Naviyuk Kane, Santee Frazier, Jimmy Santiago Baca, Ed Skoog, Denise Lowe, Jamie Figueroa, Jenn Love.

To the Institute of American Indian Arts: something cosmic led me to this campus to study creative writing. I applaud the years I spent learning from the best.

To all the unnamed lights with whom I've connected along the way ... smile. This poetry collection owes its existence to an imprinted piece of your essence. *Wado*.

Vivian Mary Carroll (Cherokee Nation) spent many years in regional theater from Alaska to New York, including teaching costuming to students of Ringling Brothers and Barnum & Bailey Combined Shows, Inc. Clown College. She worked for the Superior Court of Sacramento for twenty-three years and followed a British rock band and a country duo for many years, all the while writing and submitting for publication. She has studied at Idyllwild Arts Summer Writing Program, the Jack Kerouac School of Disembodied Poetics at Naropa University, and Writing By Writers Boulder Generative Workshop. She received her MFA at the age of seventy-two from the Institute of American Indian Arts. *Talking Leaves Scrapbook* is her first poetry collection.

Casa Urraca Press publishes creative works by authors we believe in. New Mexico and the U.S. Southwest are rich in creative and literary talent, and the rest of the world deserves to experience our perspectives. So we champion books that belong in the conversation—books with the power, compassion, and variety to bring very different people closer together.

We are proudly centered in the high desert somewhere near Abiquiú, New Mexico. Visit us at casaurracapress.com to browse our books and to register for workshops with our authors.

www.ingramcontent.com/pod-product-compliance
Lightning Source LLC
Chambersburg PA
CBHW030330141025
33974CB00004B/16